Traditional
HOLIDAY
Celebrations

Published by Barbour Publishing, Inc., P.O. Box 719, Uhrichsville, Ohio 44683, www.barbourbooks.com

Our mission is to publish and distribute inspirational products offering exceptional value and biblical encouragement to the masses.

 Member of the
Evangelical Christian
Publishers Association

Printed in China.

Traditional
HOLIDAY
Celebrations

Recipes & Inspiration for a Festive Christmas

BARBOUR

Welcome to *Traditional Holiday Celebrations*! Here you'll find a plethora of tasty recipes, festive inspiration, and ideas to make your Christmas get-togethers truly merry and bright. Each page is a stand-alone recipe card that can be easily removed from the book to add to your collection of other holiday treats; or you may choose to share some of the cards with friends and family. Consider creating the dish to give as a gift and attaching the recipe card with a bright ribbon. Or maybe slip a recipe card or two into your Christmas cards this year. You may also wish to keep the book as a whole— no matter how you use it, you can't go wrong!

Recipes are organized in colorful sections:

Eat Dessert First (The Christmas Season Is Short)

Mouthwatering Side Dishes

The Main Event: Traditional Meal Centerpieces

Sweet Treats: Cookies & Candy

Creative Traditions for All Ages

Eat Dessert First
(The Christmas Season Is Short)

For most families, traditions surrounding the holiday season are one of the many reasons this time of the year is cherished. Traditions—especially those passed down from generation to generation—bind us together in common history and shared nostalgia. What are some of the food traditions you and your family hold dear? A favorite pie just like Grandma used to make? A cake decorated in a unique and festive way? Baking together? Crafting together?

Traditions offer us a way to remember the past and celebrate the present. And maybe this year offers an opportunity to begin a new tradition with your family or friends. The sky is the limit! Use the ideas you find here as well as your own creativity, and you'll find new ways to make meaningful connections with the people you love.

> What I'd like to have for Christmas
> I can tell you in a minute
> The family all around me,
> And the home with laughter in it.
> EDGAR A. GUEST

Mystery Pecan Pie

This is a delicious variation of a traditional pecan pie.
The surprise cream cheese layer helps to balance the richness of the pecan filling.

1 unbaked piecrust for a 9-inch pie

FILLING:
1 (8 ounce) package cream cheese,
   softened
1 egg
1 teaspoon vanilla
⅓ cup sugar
¼ teaspoon salt

3 eggs
¼ cup sugar
1 cup corn syrup
1 teaspoon vanilla
1¼ cups pecans, chopped

In small bowl, beat softened cream cheese until smooth and creamy. Add

1 egg, 1 teaspoon vanilla, ⅓ cup sugar, and salt. Beat at low speed until smooth and well blended. Set aside. In another small bowl, beat 3 eggs. Stir in ¼ cup sugar, corn syrup, and 1 teaspoon vanilla; blend well. Spread cream cheese mixture in bottom of crust-lined pan. Sprinkle with chopped pecans. Gently pour corn syrup mixture over pecans. Bake at 375 degrees for 35 to 45 minutes or until center is set. If needed, cover edge of piecrust with strip of foil after 15 to 20 minutes of baking to prevent excessive browning. Cool completely. Store in refrigerator. Yield: 8 servings

Pumpkin Cream Cheese Pie

*The shortbread crust and addition of cream cheese
have made this a favorite holiday recipe.*

PECAN SHORTBREAD COOKIE CRUST:
1½ cups shortbread cookies with pecans (about 16 cookies) crushed, packed
3 tablespoons butter, melted
3 tablespoons flour

FILLING:
11 ounces cream cheese, softened
1 cup sugar
3 tablespoons flour
1 teaspoon cinnamon
¼ teaspoon nutmeg
¼ teaspoon ginger
¼ teaspoon cloves
3 eggs
1 (15 ounce) can pumpkin puree
1 tablespoon milk

CRUST: Mix all ingredients. Press firmly on bottom and up sides of ungreased 9-inch pie plate. Bake at 375 degrees for 10 to 12 minutes or until golden brown. Cool. FILLING: Beat cream cheese in large bowl on low speed until smooth; add sugar and flour. Beat until well mixed; reserve ½ cup. Add remaining ingredients except milk to original cream cheese mixture. Beat on medium speed, scraping bowl constantly, until smooth. Pour into crust. Stir milk into reserved cream cheese mixture. Spoon over pumpkin mixture. Cut through cream cheese and pumpkin mixtures with knife in S-shaped curves in one continuous motion. Turn pie plate one-fourth turn and repeat. Cover edge of crust with 2- to 3-inch strip of aluminum foil to prevent excessive browning; remove foil during last 15 minutes of baking. Bake at 375 degrees for 35 to 40 minutes or until knife inserted in center comes out clean. Cool 30 minutes. Cover loosely and refrigerate at least 4 hours.

Creamy Slow Cooker Rice Pudding

*This wonderfully creamy dessert may just take you back to your childhood.
This is an easy way to make rice pudding without all the
stirring and watching of the stove method.*

7 cups milk
1 cup sugar
1 cup uncooked long-grain white rice
1 cup raisins
1½ cups boiling water

3 eggs, lightly beaten
1 (12 ounce) can evaporated milk
¼ teaspoon salt
2 teaspoons vanilla extract
Cinnamon to taste

In large slow cooker, combine milk, sugar, and rice. Cook on high for 4
hours or low for 8 hours. In small bowl, combine raisins and boiling water;
allow to plump for 10 minutes. Drain well. In small bowl, combine eggs,

evaporated milk, salt, vanilla, and drained raisins. Temper by adding 1 cup hot rice mixture to egg mixture and mix. Stir egg mixture into rice mixture and continue cooking on low an additional 30 minutes. Pour into 9x13-inch dish and cover with plastic wrap, folding back the corners to allow the steam to escape. When pudding has cooled to room temperature, remove plastic wrap and sprinkle surface of pudding with cinnamon. Cover tightly (with fresh wrap) and refrigerate 8 hours or overnight before serving.

Notes

....

....

....

Carrot Cranberry Cake

For people who like carrot cake but don't care for raisins, the cranberries are a nice option. Topped with yummy cream cheese frosting, it's moist and delicious.

1¾ cups flour
2 teaspoons baking soda
2 teaspoons baking powder
2 teaspoons cinnamon
½ teaspoon salt
½ teaspoon allspice
¼ teaspoon ground ginger
1½ cups sugar

1 cup mayonnaise or sour cream
3 eggs
1 tablespoon brandy or water
2 cups carrots, shredded
1 (8 ounce) can crushed pineapple in
   juice, undrained
½ cup pecans or walnuts, chopped
½ cup dried cranberries

Mix flour, baking soda, baking powder, cinnamon, salt, allspice, and ginger;

set aside. Beat sugar, mayonnaise, and eggs in large bowl with electric mixer on medium speed, scraping bowl occasionally, until blended. Beat in brandy. Gradually beat in flour mixture until batter is smooth. Stir in carrots, pineapple, nuts, and cranberries. Pour into three 8-inch round greased pans. Bake at 350 degrees for 30 to 35 minutes or until toothpick inserted in center comes out clean. Cool 10 minutes; remove from pans to wire rack. Cool completely. Fill layers and frost sides and top of cake with Cream Cheese Frosting (recipe follows). Garnish with sugared cranberries and orange peel if desired.

Cream Cheese Frosting

6 ounces cream cheese, softened
3 tablespoons butter, softened

1 teaspoon vanilla
2½ to 3 cups powdered sugar

Beat cream cheese until smooth; add butter and vanilla. Mix well. Gradually beat in powdered sugar on low speed until smooth and spreadable.

Old-Fashioned Graham Cracker Pudding

Old-fashioned cooked pudding, layered with whipped cream, graham cracker crumbs, and bananas. This is one dessert that doesn't stay around long.

PUDDING LAYER:
5 cups milk, divided
½ cup flour
1 cup brown sugar
4 egg yolks, beaten
1 teaspoon vanilla

BANANA LAYER:
2 bananas, peeled and sliced

GRAHAM CRACKER CRUMB LAYER:
12 graham crackers, crushed
2 tablespoons butter, melted
1 tablespoon brown sugar

WHIPPED CREAM:
1 cup heavy whipping cream
¼ cup powdered sugar
1 teaspoon vanilla

PUDDING: In medium saucepan, heat 4 cups milk. In medium bowl, combine flour, 1 cup brown sugar, and egg yolks; whisk until smooth. Stir in 1 cup cold milk. Mix well. Temper egg mixture by adding 1 cup hot milk to egg mixture; stir until well mixed. Stir egg mixture into hot milk, stirring constantly. Cook until thickened. Remove from heat; add vanilla. Place piece of plastic wrap on top of pudding to keep from forming film. Refrigerate until cooled. WHIPPED CREAM: In medium grease-free mixing bowl, whip heavy whipping cream until stiff peaks form. Add powdered sugar and vanilla. Beat until mixed and stiff peaks form again. Refrigerate until needed. When pudding is cool, stir in ½ cup whipped cream. GRAHAM CRACKER CRUMBS: Mix cracker crumb ingredients. Layer crumbs with pudding and banana slices in serving bowl. End layers with remaining whipped cream, sprinkled with crumbs and banana slices. Serve.

Caramel Pear Crumb Pie

6 cups ripe pears, peeled and thinly sliced
(about 6 medium pears)
1 tablespoon lemon juice
½ cup plus 3 tablespoons sugar, divided
2 tablespoons quick-cooking tapioca
¾ teaspoon cinnamon
¼ teaspoon salt
¼ teaspoon nutmeg

1 (9 inch) unbaked pastry shell
¾ cup old-fashioned oats
1 tablespoon flour
¼ cup cold butter, cubed
18 caramels
5 tablespoons milk
¼ cup pecans, chopped

In large bowl, combine pears and lemon juice. In another bowl, combine ½ cup sugar, tapioca, cinnamon, salt, and nutmeg. Add to pears; stir gently. Let stand for 15 minutes. Pour into pastry shell. In bowl, combine oats, flour, and

3 tablespoons sugar. Cut in butter until crumbly. Sprinkle over pears. Bake at 400 degrees for 45 minutes. Meanwhile, in saucepan over low heat, melt caramels with milk. Stir until smooth; add pecans. Drizzle over pie. Bake an additional 8 to 10 minutes or until crust is golden brown and filling is bubbly. Cool on wire rack.

Notes

....

....

....

....

Praline Pumpkin Torte

PRALINE:
¾ cup brown sugar
⅓ cup butter
3 tablespoons heavy whipping cream
¾ cup pecans, chopped

TOPPING:
1¾ cups heavy whipping cream
¼ cup powdered sugar
¼ teaspoon vanilla
Additional chopped pecans

CAKE:
4 eggs
1⅔ cups sugar
1 cup canola oil
2 cups canned pumpkin
1 teaspoon vanilla
2 cups flour
2 teaspoons baking powder
2 teaspoons pumpkin pie spice
1 teaspoon baking soda
1 teaspoon salt

Preheat oven to 350 degrees. **PRALINE:** In heavy saucepan, combine brown sugar, butter, and cream. Cook and stir over low heat until sugar is dissolved. Pour into two well-greased 9-inch round cake pans. Sprinkle with pecans; cool. CAKE: In large bowl, beat eggs, sugar, and oil. Add pumpkin and vanilla. In another bowl, combine flour, baking powder, pumpkin pie spice, baking soda, and salt; gradually add to pumpkin mixture just until blended. Carefully spoon batter over brown sugar mixture. Bake at 350 degrees for 30 to 35 minutes or until toothpick inserted near center comes out clean. Cool for 5 minutes; remove from pans to wire racks to cool completely. TOPPING: In small bowl, beat cream until it begins to thicken. Add powdered sugar and vanilla; beat until stiff peaks form. Place cake layer praline side up on serving plate. Spread two-thirds of whipped cream mixture over cake. Top with second cake layer and remaining whipped cream. Sprinkle with additional pecans if desired. Store in refrigerator.

Gingerbread with Warm Lemon Sauce

GINGERBREAD:

½ cup sugar
½ cup butter, softened
1 egg
1 cup molasses
2½ cups flour
1½ teaspoons baking soda

½ teaspoon salt
1½ teaspoons cinnamon
¾ teaspoon ginger
¾ teaspoon cloves
1 cup hot water

LEMON SAUCE:

¾ cup sugar
2 teaspoons cornstarch
Dash of salt
Dash of nutmeg
1 cup water

2 egg yolks, beaten
2 tablespoons butter
2 tablespoons lemon juice
½ teaspoon lemon peel, grated

GINGERBREAD: In large bowl, cream sugar and butter. Beat in egg and molasses. In separate bowl, combine flour, baking soda, salt, cinnamon, ginger, and cloves. Add to molasses mixture alternately with hot water, just until blended. Pour into greased 9x9-inch baking pan. Bake at 350 degrees for 50 to 60 minutes or until toothpick inserted near center comes out clean.

LEMON SAUCE: In saucepan, combine first five ingredients until smooth. Bring to a boil; cook and stir for 1 to 2 minutes or until thickened.

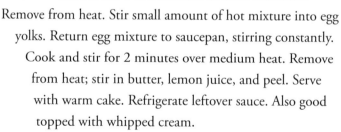

Remove from heat. Stir small amount of hot mixture into egg yolks. Return egg mixture to saucepan, stirring constantly. Cook and stir for 2 minutes over medium heat. Remove from heat; stir in butter, lemon juice, and peel. Serve with warm cake. Refrigerate leftover sauce. Also good topped with whipped cream.

Heirloom Fruitcake

⅓ cup butter, softened (do not substitute)
3 tablespoons brown sugar
2 eggs, lightly beaten
3 tablespoons honey
½ cup flour
½ teaspoon salt
½ teaspoon baking powder

⅛ teaspoon allspice
¼ teaspoon cinnamon
2 tablespoons half-and-half
1 cup raisins
1 cup dates, chopped
6 ounces dried apricots, finely chopped
3 cups pecan halves

Cream butter, sugar, eggs, and honey in mixing bowl. Combine dry ingredients; add to creamed mixture alternately with half-and-half. Beat in raisins, dates, apricots, and pecans. Pour into two greased and floured loaf pans. Place pans on middle rack of oven; place shallow pan of hot water on lowest rack. Bake at 300 degrees for 60 to 65 minutes or until toothpick inserted near the center comes out clean. Cool completely in pan. Loosen edges with knife and remove from pan. Store in airtight container in refrigerator.

Notes

....

....

....

....

....

Almond Legend Cake

CAKE:

1 (2 ounce) package slivered almonds, chopped
⅓ cup butter, softened
⅓ cup shortening
1¼ cups sugar
3 eggs, separated
1 teaspoon lemon rind, grated
2 tablespoons lemon juice
1 teaspoon vanilla

1 teaspoon almond extract
2⅓ cups flour
2 teaspoons baking powder
¼ teaspoon baking soda
¾ teaspoon salt
¾ cup milk
½ teaspoon cream of tartar
¼ cup sugar
1 whole almond

APRICOT GLAZE:

½ cup apricot preserves

1 tablespoon orange juice

CAKE: Sprinkle chopped almonds into well-greased 10-inch Bundt pan; set aside. Cream butter and shortening; add 1¼ cups sugar and beat until light and fluffy. Add egg yolks and beat well. Add lemon rind, lemon juice, vanilla, and almond extract. Mix well. Combine flour, baking powder, soda, and salt. Add to creamed mixture alternately with milk until well blended. Set batter aside. Beat egg whites and cream of tartar until foamy. Add ¼ cup sugar, beating until stiff peaks form; fold egg whites into batter. Pour batter into prepared pan. Press whole almond just below surface of batter. Bake at 350 degrees for 50 to 55 minutes or until wooden toothpick inserted in center comes out clean. Cool in pan 10 minutes; remove from pan and let cool completely on wire rack. APRICOT GLAZE: Heat preserves, and strain through a sieve. Add orange juice; stir well. Drizzle over cooled cake. Cake texture and taste are very similar to batter bread.

Pecan Tassies

CRUST:
1 (3 ounce) package cream cheese, softened

½ cup butter, softened
1 cup flour

FILLING:
1 egg
¾ cup dark brown sugar, packed
1 tablespoon butter, melted

Pinch salt
1 teaspoon vanilla extract
⅔ cup pecans, chopped

CRUST: In mixing bowl, beat cream cheese until smooth. Add butter; mix well. Blend in flour. Wrap dough in plastic wrap and chill for 1 hour. Shape into 1-inch balls; press into bottom and up sides of greased mini muffin cups.

FILLING: Beat egg in small mixing bowl. Add brown sugar, butter, salt, and vanilla; mix well. Stir in pecans. Spoon into mini muffin cups and bake at 325 degrees for 20 to 25 minutes. Cool in pan on wire rack.

Notes

....

....

....

....

....

Pecan Tarts

CRUST:
1 cup butter, softened
6 ounces cream cheese, softened

2½ cups flour
¼ teaspoon salt

FILLING:
3 eggs, slightly beaten
1½ cups brown sugar
¾ cup light corn syrup
3 tablespoons butter, melted

⅛ teaspoon salt
¾ teaspoon vanilla
½ cup pecans, chopped

CRUST: Combine softened butter and cream cheese. In separate bowl, mix flour and salt. Add flour mixture to butter mixture and combine until blended. Chill dough 10 minutes. Shape dough into 1-inch balls; press in bottom and up sides of greased mini muffin cups. FILLING: Mix eggs, brown sugar, corn syrup, butter, salt, and vanilla. Place small amount of nuts in bottom of each tart. Add filling and bake at 350 degrees for 18 to 20 minutes.

Notes

....

....

....

....

....

Very Berry Cobbler

1½ cups sugar
½ cup cornstarch
4 cups fresh or frozen red raspberries
4 cups fresh or frozen blueberries
4 cups fresh or frozen blackberries
¼ cup lemon juice
1½ cups flour
½ cup brown sugar
1½ teaspoons baking powder

½ teaspoon salt
½ teaspoon nutmeg
½ cup butter
⅓ cup hot water
Sugar
Nutmeg
Whipped cream or ice cream, if desired
Orange zest, if desired

In large saucepan, mix sugar and cornstarch. Add berries and lemon juice; toss until evenly coated. Heat berries to boiling. Boil 1 minute, stirring constantly.

Spoon berry mixture into greased 9x13-inch baking dish. In large mixing bowl, mix flour, brown sugar, baking powder, salt, and nutmeg. Cut in butter using pastry blender or crisscrossing two knives until mixture resembles coarse crumbs. Stir in hot water until mixture forms soft dough; do not overmix. Spoon dough onto berry mixture. Sprinkle with additional sugar and nutmeg. Bake at 400 degrees for 35 to 40 minutes or until top is golden brown. Serve warm with whipped cream and garnish with orange zest if desired. Also delicious served with vanilla ice cream.

Notes

....

....

....

Chocolate Caramel Pecan Cheesecake

CRUST:
2 cups vanilla wafer crumbs

6 tablespoons butter, melted

CARAMEL FILLING:
1 (14 ounce) bag caramels
¼ cup milk

1 cup pecans, chopped

CHEESECAKE:
2 (8 ounce) packages cream cheese,
   softened
½ cup sugar
1 teaspoon vanilla

2 eggs
4 squares semisweet chocolate,
   melted and cooled slightly

CRUST: Mix crumbs and butter together and press on bottom and 1½ inches up sides of 9-inch springform pan. Bake for 8 to 10 minutes. CARAMEL FILLING: In small saucepan, combine caramels and milk over low heat, stirring constantly, until melted. Pour over crust. Top with pecans. CHEESECAKE: In mixing bowl, beat cream cheese until smooth, scraping bowl occasionally. Add sugar and vanilla and beat until well blended. Add eggs, one at a time, mixing at low speed after each addition, just until blended. Fold in melted chocolate; pour over pecans. Place glass baking dish with several inches of water on lower oven rack beneath cheesecake to help prevent cracking. Bake at 325 degrees for 45 to 50 minutes or until center is almost set. Open oven door and let cheesecake cool 1 hour. Run knife or metal spatula around rim of pan to loosen cake; cool before removing rim of pan. Refrigerate 4 hours or overnight.

Mouthwatering Side Dishes

Everybody has their favorite side dish when it comes to a holiday feast. Usually side dishes are chosen to complement whatever main dish is being served, but why eliminate a beloved side just because it doesn't "fit" in the vast scheme of the meal? If you're up for a little shake-up of your traditional meal, consider planning a "sides only" spread. Invite guests to bring their favorite side dish—from rolls and salads to mashed potatoes and green bean casserole—and enjoy just the trimmings (but a lot of them!). You might just find a new favorite to add to your traditional Christmas dinner.

When candles light
December night
And Christmas joy unfolds,
Bright dreams abound
As peace surrounds
The gifts this season holds.

So gather 'round
And hear the sound
Of singing 'round the earth
The heavens ring
When we all sing
Proclaiming Jesus' birth.

UNKNOWN

Sweet Potato Casserole

Many folks think it's not Christmas without this sweet dessertlike dish.
The crunchy pecan topping makes it irresistible.
Even people who don't like sweet potatoes enjoy this side.

POTATOES:

4½ cups sweet potatoes, cooked and
   mashed
½ cup butter, melted
⅓ cup evaporated milk

1 cup sugar
1 teaspoon vanilla
2 eggs, beaten

TOPPING:

1 cup light brown sugar
½ cup flour

⅓ cup butter
1 cup pecans, chopped

POTATOES: In large bowl, mix together mashed sweet potatoes, ½ cup butter, milk, sugar, vanilla, and eggs. Spread sweet potato mixture into greased 9x13-inch baking dish. TOPPING: In small bowl, mix together brown sugar and flour. Cut in ⅓ cup butter until mixture is crumbly; stir in pecans. Sprinkle pecan mixture over sweet potatoes. Bake at 350 degrees for 25 minutes, or until golden brown.

Notes

Roasted Brussels Sprouts and Carrots

1 tablespoon salt
1 pound brussels sprouts, trimmed and
  halved lengthwise
1 cup fresh baby carrots, halved
  lengthwise
2 tablespoons olive oil
Sea salt to taste

Ground black pepper to taste
4 slices bacon, chopped
1 shallot, chopped
7 baby bella mushrooms, chopped
1 clove garlic, minced
¼ cup cream sherry
½ cup heavy cream

Dissolve 1 tablespoon salt in enough water to cover brussels sprouts in bowl; soak sprouts in the salty water for 1 hour. Drain off water; toss sprouts and carrots in olive oil, sea salt, and black pepper to coat thoroughly. Place bacon in large, deep skillet, and cook over medium-high heat, stirring occasionally, until just beginning to brown at the edges, 5 to 8 minutes. Reduce heat to medium; stir in shallot and mushrooms, then cook until shallots turn translucent, about 5 more minutes. Sprinkle in garlic and cook 1 minute, then stir in sherry and cream until well combined. Bring mixture to a boil; stir until reduced by half. The thickened sauce should coat the back of a spoon. While sauce is cooking, lay brussels sprouts and carrots cut sides down, onto baking sheet, and bake at 475 degrees until the sprouts and carrots are browned, about 15 minutes. Transfer browned sprouts to sauce, toss to coat, and season to taste with salt and black pepper.

Party Cranberry Salad

Here is a refreshing salad perfect for any holiday gathering.

SALAD:
- 1 (20 ounce) can crushed pineapple, drained, juice reserved
- 1 (3 ounce) package cranberry-flavored gelatin mix
- 1 (3 ounce) package raspberry-flavored gelatin mix
- 1 cup cold water
- 2 (16 ounce) cans whole cranberry sauce
- 1 apple, peeled, cored, and chopped
- ½ cup walnuts, chopped

TOPPING:
- 1 (8 ounce) package cream cheese, softened
- 1 cup sour cream
- ½ cup sugar
- 1 teaspoon vanilla

SALAD: In saucepan, combine reserved pineapple juice and enough water to make 1 cup. Bring liquid to a boil and add cranberry and raspberry gelatins; stir until dissolved. Add cold water and cool to room temperature. In mixing bowl, combine pineapple, cranberry sauce, apple, and nuts. Add to gelatin and mix well. Pour into 9x13-inch glass pan and refrigerate until set. TOPPING: Beat cream cheese until smooth and creamy. Add sour cream, sugar, and vanilla. Mix well. Spread topping on firm gelatin. Refrigerate until ready to serve.

Notes

Mashed Potatoes

Here's a traditional take on a family favorite side,
plus a savory garlic recipe on the other side of this card.

6 medium russet potatoes,
  peeled and quartered
¾ cup warm milk

¼ cup butter
¾ teaspoon salt
2 tablespoons butter

Place potatoes in saucepan with 3 inches of water. Cover and bring to a boil;
cook for 20 to 25 minutes or until fork tender. Drain well. Return to saucepan.
Beat with electric mixer until well mashed. Scrape pan. Add milk, butter, and
salt; beat until light and fluffy. In small skillet, brown 2 tablespoons butter.
Spoon mashed potatoes into bowl and pour browned butter over top.

Garlic Mashed Potatoes

8 medium red potatoes, unpeeled,
  quartered
¼ cup butter
4 to 5 cloves garlic, peeled and minced*

1 cup warm milk
Salt to taste
¼ cup parmesan cheese, grated

Place potatoes in large saucepan with 2 inches of water. Cover and bring to a boil. Reduce heat; cover and simmer for 20 to 25 minutes or until potatoes are very tender. In small skillet, melt butter; add minced garlic and sauté on low until golden brown. Add milk and heat until warm. Drain potatoes well. Return potatoes to saucepan and mash. Scrape sides of pan; add the milk mixture and salt; mash. Stir in parmesan cheese. *You can also roast one bulb of garlic drizzled with olive oil and wrapped in foil. Bake for 25 to 30 minutes at 350 degrees. Let cool and squeeze garlic out. Use in place of minced garlic.

Baked Corn Casserole

This card includes two corn dishes. The first one is more solid and cakelike, the second more of a pudding consistency. Take your pick. Both are delicious!

1 (16 ounce) can whole kernel corn
1 (16 ounce) can cream-style corn
1 cup sour cream

½ cup butter, melted
1 egg, beaten
1 (8.5 ounce) box corn muffin mix

Mix all ingredients together. Pour into greased 2-quart baking dish; cover and bake at 350 degrees for 45 minutes. Uncover and bake 15 minutes longer or until top is golden brown.

Corn Pudding

5 eggs
⅓ cup butter, melted
¼ cup sugar
½ cup milk

4 tablespoons cornstarch
1 (15.25 ounce) can whole kernel corn
2 (14.75 ounce) cans cream-style corn
Nutmeg

In large bowl, lightly beat eggs. Add melted butter and sugar. Whisk together milk and cornstarch; add to egg mixture. Stir in corn and creamed corn. Blend well. Pour mixture into greased shallow 2-quart casserole dish. Sprinkle with nutmeg. Bake at 400 degrees for 1 hour.

Cauliflower Bake

WHITE SAUCE:
4 tablespoons butter
4 tablespoons flour
1 teaspoon salt
¼ teaspoon pepper

2 cups milk
1 large head cauliflower
3 hard-boiled eggs, diced

TOPPING:
2 tablespoons butter
1 cup bread, cubed

¼ cup swiss cheese, grated

WHITE SAUCE: Melt butter in saucepan; add flour, salt, and pepper. Stir until well blended; cook 1 minute on medium heat. Slowly add milk; cook, stirring constantly, until mixture thickens. Break head of cauliflower into florets and cook in salt water; drain. Alternate layers of cauliflower, diced eggs, and white sauce in greased 2-quart baking dish. TOPPING: In small skillet, melt butter; add bread cubes; toss and fry until toasted. Top cauliflower with grated cheese and toasted bread crumbs. Bake at 375 degrees for 25 minutes.

Notes

Nutty Rice Pilaf

¼ cup butter, melted
⅓ cup onion, chopped
1 cup long-grain rice, uncooked
¼ cup raisins, divided
2 cups water
2 chicken-flavored bouillon cubes
⅛ teaspoon salt

⅛ teaspoon pepper
Pinch of thyme
Pinch of oregano
1 tablespoon vegetable oil
¼ cup salted peanuts, coarsely chopped
¼ cup plus 1 tablespoon coarsely chopped
    almonds, toasted and divided

In medium skillet, heat butter; sauté onion until tender. Add rice; cook over low heat until lightly browned, stirring frequently. Pour into lightly greased 1½-quart baking dish; sprinkle with 3 tablespoons raisins. Combine water and bouillon cubes in small saucepan; bring to a boil. Stir in salt, pepper, thyme, and oregano; pour over rice. Cover and bake at 350 degrees for 25 minutes or until rice is tender. In saucepan, heat oil; sauté chopped peanuts. Stir 2 tablespoons peanuts and ¼ cup almonds into rice. Garnish pilaf with remaining raisins, peanuts, and almonds.

Notes

Harvard Beets

The color of this beet dish adds lovely color to any meal.
It has a sweet, tangy sauce that is easy to make.

⅔ cup sugar
4 teaspoons cornstarch
Dash ground cloves
Dash cinnamon
⅓ cup white vinegar

2 (15 ounce) cans sliced beets, drained,
   juice reserved
3 tablespoons butter
¼ teaspoon salt
¼ teaspoon pepper

In saucepan, combine sugar, cornstarch, cloves, and cinnamon. Stir in vinegar and ⅓ cup reserved beet juice. Bring to a boil and cook for 5 minutes. Add beets to liquid and simmer for 20 minutes over low heat or until sauce is thickened and red beets are heated through. Stir in butter, salt, and pepper and remove from heat. Serve warm or chilled.

Notes

Poppy Seed Apple Salad

Poppy seeds give this apple salad a unique flavor.

1 (20 ounce) can pineapple chunks
¼ cup butter
¼ cup sugar
1 tablespoon lemon juice
2 tablespoons cornstarch
2 tablespoons cold water
1 cup mayonnaise

8 cups tart apples, chopped
¼ cup celery, chopped
2 cups green grapes
2 teaspoons poppy seeds
¾ cup pecans or walnuts, chopped
1 banana, sliced

Drain pineapple, reserving juice; set pineapple aside. Place juice in saucepan; add butter, sugar, and lemon juice. Bring to a boil. Combine cornstarch and cold water until smooth; add to saucepan, stirring constantly. Return to a boil; cook and stir for 2 minutes. Chill. Stir in mayonnaise. In large bowl, combine pineapple, apples, celery, grapes, poppy seeds, and cooked mixture. Fold in nuts and sliced banana just before serving.

Notes

Apple Pear Cranberry Sauce

Consider using this as a side to meat such as turkey or pork.

3 (3 inch) cinnamon sticks
4 whole allspice berries
4 whole cloves
3 cups fresh cranberries
1¼ cups orange juice

2 apples, peeled, cored, and diced
2 pears, peeled, cored, and diced
1½ cups white sugar
½ cup brown sugar

Place cinnamon sticks, allspice berries, and cloves onto center of 8-inch square piece of cheesecloth. Gather together edges of cheesecloth and tie with kitchen twine to secure. Place sachet in large saucepan along with cranberries and orange juice. Bring to a boil over high heat and cook until cranberries begin to burst, about 10 minutes. Stir in apples, pears, white sugar, and brown sugar. Return to boil, then reduce heat to medium-low, and simmer about 25 minutes, until apples and pears are slightly soft. Remove and discard spice sachet. Scrape sauce into bowl; cover and refrigerate overnight. Serve cold.

Notes

New Green Bean Casserole

Classic taste with a modern twist. Fresh ingredients update this well-loved tradition. If fresh green beans aren't available, use the whole frozen variety.

3 pounds green beans, trimmed and cut in half
4 large shallots, divided
1 tablespoon olive oil
1½ cups coarse bread crumbs
1 teaspoon fresh thyme leaves, chopped
½ teaspoon salt, divided
½ teaspoon freshly ground black pepper, divided
3 cups milk
3 tablespoons butter
¼ cup flour
⅛ teaspoon nutmeg, freshly grated
½ cup parmesan cheese, freshly grated

Heat covered 8-quart saucepan of salted water to boiling on high heat. Add green beans and cook 6 minutes or until bright green and just tender. Drain well; transfer to shallow 3-quart glass or ceramic baking dish. Finely chop 2 shallots. Thinly slice remaining shallots; set aside. In 12-inch skillet, heat oil on medium heat until hot. Add chopped shallots and cook 4 to 7 minutes or until browned and tender, stirring occasionally. Add bread crumbs and cook 2 minutes or until dry and golden. Stir in thyme, ¼ teaspoon salt, and ¼ teaspoon freshly ground black pepper. In microwave-safe measuring cup, microwave milk on high 4 minutes or until milk is warm. Meanwhile in same skillet, melt butter on medium heat. Add sliced shallots and cook 5 minutes or until golden brown and tender, stirring occasionally. Add flour and cook 2 minutes, stirring. Gradually pour milk into flour mixture in slow steady stream, stirring constantly; heat to boiling, stirring. Stir 2 minutes longer or until thickened (mixture should have the consistency of heavy cream). Stir in nutmeg, ¼ teaspoon salt, and ¼ teaspoon freshly ground black pepper. Pour sauce over green beans; gently stir until green beans are evenly coated. Stir parmesan cheese into bread crumb mixture; spread evenly over green bean mixture in casserole. Bake at 350 degrees for 30 minutes or until bread crumbs are golden brown and sauce is bubbly.

Broccoli Salad

1 pound maple bacon
¾ cup blanched slivered almonds
1 cup mayonnaise
¼ cup sugar
1 tablespoon distilled white vinegar

2 large heads fresh broccoli, chopped
¾ cup chopped celery
¼ cup green onion, minced
¼ cup red onion, diced
1½ cups seedless grapes, halved

Place bacon in large skillet. Cook, turning frequently, over medium-high heat until evenly browned. Cool and crumble. Refrigerate until time to use. Spread slivered almonds on cookie sheet. Bake at 350 degrees for approximately 12 to 14 minutes or until lightly browned, turning once during toasting. Cool. In small bowl, mix together mayonnaise, sugar, and vinegar. Set aside. In large bowl, combine broccoli, celery, green onion, red onion, grapes, and toasted almonds. Toss with mayonnaise dressing. Chill for several hours in the refrigerator. Add crumbled bacon just before serving.

Notes

Autumn Squash Casserole

Here's a casserole with a wonderful mix of flavors and textures.

3 pounds butternut squash, peeled,
   seeded, and cut into ¾-inch chunks
¼ cup butter
1 tablespoon brown sugar
¼ teaspoon salt
Dash white pepper
1½ tablespoons butter
6 cups apples, peeled and diced

¼ cup dried cranberries
¼ cup sugar
1½ cups cornflakes cereal,
   coarsely crushed
½ cup pecans, chopped
½ cup brown sugar
2 tablespoons butter, melted

Place cut-up squash in medium saucepan and cover with 2 inches of water.
 Bring to a boil; lower heat and cook until squash is tender, about 15 minutes.

Drain; beat with hand mixer until mashed. Add ¼ cup butter, 1 tablespoon brown sugar, salt, and white pepper. Heat 1½ tablespoons butter in large skillet over low heat. Stir in diced apples and cranberries; sprinkle with sugar. Cover and cook over low heat until barely tender, about 5 minutes, stirring occasionally. Spread apple mixture in greased 3-quart casserole dish. Spoon mashed squash evenly over apples. Stir together cornflakes, pecans, ½ cup brown sugar, and 2 tablespoons melted butter. Sprinkle cornflake mixture evenly over squash. Bake at 350 degrees for 15 minutes or until heated through.

Corn Bread Stuffing

½ cup butter
2 cups celery, chopped
1 cup onion, chopped
6 cups cubed day-old corn bread
2 cups fresh bread crumbs
1 tablespoon dried sage

1 tablespoon poultry seasoning
½ cup egg substitute
1 cup chicken broth
1 turkey (10 to 12 pounds)
Melted butter

Heat butter in skillet; sauté celery and onion until tender. Place in large bowl with corn bread, bread crumbs, sage, and poultry seasoning. Combine egg substitute and broth; add to corn bread mixture, stirring gently to mix. Just before baking turkey, stuff body cavity and inside the neck with dressing*. Skewer or fasten openings. Tie drumsticks together. Place on rack in roasting pan. Brush with melted butter. Bake at 325 degrees for 3½ to 4 hours or until meat thermometer reads 180 degrees for the turkey and 165 degrees for the stuffing. When turkey begins to brown, cover lightly with tent of aluminum foil. When turkey is done, allow to stand 20 minutes. Remove all dressing to serving bowl. *Dressing may be prepared as above and baked in greased 2-quart casserole dish. Cover and bake at 400 degrees for 20 minutes. Uncover and bake 10 minutes longer or until lightly browned.

Notes

Cinnamon Candy Apple Salad

The cinnamon candies add a spicy flavor to this apple salad.
It looks nice served as an individual side dish plated on a lettuce leaf.

1 cup water
⅓ cup cinnamon red hot candies
1 (3 ounce) package cherry-flavored
  gelatin
¾ cup cold water

½ cup tart apples, diced
½ cup celery, chopped
½ cup walnuts, chopped
½ cup red grapes, halved

In small saucepan, mix water and cinnamon candy. Bring to a boil, stirring occasionally. Remove from heat and continue to stir until candy is totally dissolved. In medium bowl, add boiling water to cherry gelatin and stir until well dissolved; then add ¾ cup cold water. Allow mixture to begin to set in the refrigerator. When it has begun to gel, mix in apples, celery, walnuts, and grapes. Pour gelatin mixture into decorative mold or serving bowl and refrigerate overnight to set.

Notes

The Main Event:
Traditional Meal Centerpieces

An elegant, seated dinner party is one of the longtime traditions of the season that has been largely lost in these days of more spontaneous and casual entertaining. Once in a while, however, people love to attend an event where the hostess has obviously pulled out all the stops. Create a guest list, plan the menu (main course, starch, vegetable, bread, beverage, and dessert). Sit down with pen, paper, and recipes and build your shopping list one recipe at a time. To plan your table setting and centerpiece, make sure you have enough chairs, the right size tablecloth, coordinating cloth napkins, and napkin rings. A low centerpiece is crucial, as your guests will be doing most of their visiting while seated at the table and should be able to see each other easily. Fresh-cut flowers, floating candles among flower petals or cranberries, or short evergreen sprays with bright Christmas bulbs attached are all good choices.

The night of the dinner, don't rush things. As guests arrive, allow them to chat and warm up over appetizers. Plan to serve dinner about thirty minutes after everyone gets there.

Other tips:

- Set the table the evening before, so if you're missing something crucial you'll know ahead of time.

- Choose relaxing Christmas music and have it ready to turn on when guests arrive.

- Light candles, sit down, and close your eyes for ten minutes ahead of guests' arrival. If you're rested and relaxed, they will be, too.

Holiday Ham with Pineapple Glaze

1 (12 to 14 pound) fully cooked, bone-in
  ham, spiral cut or thinly sliced
2 (6 ounce) cans pineapple juice
1 (20 ounce) can crushed pineapple,
  undrained

2 cups brown sugar, packed
20 to 30 whole cloves
¼ cup golden raisins

Place ham in roasting pan. Slowly pour pineapple juice over ham so it runs between slices. Spoon crushed pineapple over ham. Sprinkle with brown sugar and cloves. Add raisins to pan juices. Cover and refrigerate overnight. Discard cloves. Cover and bake ham at 325 degrees for 1½ to 2 hours or until meat thermometer reads 140 degrees, basting every 20 minutes.

Honey Mustard Glazed Ham

1 (10 pound) fully cooked, bone-in ham
1¼ cups dark brown sugar, packed
⅓ cup pineapple juice
⅓ cup honey

½ medium orange, juiced and zested
2 tablespoons dijon mustard
¼ teaspoon ground cloves

Place ham in roasting pan. In small saucepan, combine brown sugar, pineapple juice, honey, orange juice, orange zest, dijon mustard, and ground cloves. Bring to a boil, reduce heat, and simmer for 5 to 10 minutes. Set aside. Bake ham at 325 degrees uncovered for 2 hours. Remove ham from oven; brush with glaze. Bake for an additional 30 to 45 minutes, brushing ham with glaze every 10 minutes.

Apple-Stuffed Pork Chops

*These extra-thick stuffed pork chops will quickly become a family favorite.
The sweet apple stuffing is a nice complement to the saltiness of the chops.
You can make gravy from the pan juices and serve with mashed potatoes.*

¼ cup butter
1 tablespoon onion, chopped
3 cups soft bread cubes
2 cups apples, finely chopped
¼ cup celery, finely chopped

2 teaspoons fresh parsley, minced
¾ teaspoon salt, divided
6 pork loin chops (1½ inches thick)
⅛ teaspoon pepper
1 tablespoon cooking oil

Heat butter in skillet; sauté onion in butter until tender. Remove from heat;
add bread cubes, apples, celery, parsley, and ¼ teaspoon salt. Toss until well
mixed. Cut large pocket in side of each pork chop; sprinkle the inside and

outside with pepper and remaining salt. Spoon stuffing loosely into pockets. In large skillet, heat oil; brown pork chops on both sides. Place pork chops in large greased baking pan. Cover and bake at 350 degrees for 30 minutes. Uncover and bake 30 minutes longer or until meat juices run clear.

Notes

Ham and Scalloped Potatoes

5 tablespoons butter
1 small onion, diced
5 tablespoons flour
2¼ cups milk
½ teaspoon pepper
½ teaspoon dry mustard
1 teaspoon garlic powder
1 teaspoon onion powder

1 teaspoon salt
Pinch cayenne pepper
5 to 6 medium potatoes, peeled and
    thinly sliced
1 cup fully cooked ham, cubed
¼ cup parmesan cheese
Paprika (optional)

In large skillet, melt butter over medium heat. Add diced onion; sauté until tender. Stir in flour until crumbly; cook 1 minute longer. Slowly whisk in milk, stirring constantly. Continue cooking until mixture thickens. Remove from heat and stir in pepper, dry mustard, garlic powder, onion powder, salt, and cayenne pepper. In greased 2-quart casserole, layer potato slices, milk mixture, and ham cubes, ending with milk mixture. Sprinkle with parmesan cheese and paprika. Bake at 375 degrees for 1 hour.

Notes

Easy Meat Loaf

This is a basic meat loaf with no fancy additions. Tradition at its finest.

MEAT LOAF:
1½ pounds ground beef
¾ cup quick oatmeal
2 eggs, beaten
¼ cup onion, finely chopped

1 cup tomato juice
1½ teaspoons salt
¼ teaspoon pepper

SAUCE:
⅓ cup ketchup
1½ teaspoons mustard

¼ cup brown sugar
2 tablespoons barbecue sauce

MEAT LOAF: Combine beef, oatmeal, eggs, onion, tomato juice, salt, and pepper; mix thoroughly. Pack firmly into lightly greased 5x9-inch loaf pan, or form into loaf and place in lightly greased 9x13-inch baking dish. SAUCE: Mix sauce ingredients together and pour over meat loaf. Bake at 350 degrees for 1 hour. Let stand for 5 minutes before slicing.

Notes

Stuffed Cornish Hens with Apricot Glaze

CORNISH HEN:
2 tablespoons butter
½ cup celery, chopped
¼ cup fresh mushrooms, sliced
1 (6 ounce) package fast-cooking long-grain and wild rice mix
1 (14.5 ounce) can reduced-sodium chicken broth

¼ cup water
⅔ cup water chestnuts, sliced, chopped
½ cup dried cranberries
½ cup green onions, chopped
2 tablespoons reduced-sodium soy sauce
5 cornish game hens

APRICOT GLAZE:
2 tablespoons butter, melted
½ cup apricot preserves
2 tablespoons honey

2 tablespoons grated onion
¼ teaspoon ground nutmeg

CORNISH HEN: In large saucepan coated with nonstick cooking spray, heat butter; cook celery and mushrooms in butter until tender. Stir in rice; cook 1 minute longer. Stir in contents of rice seasoning packet, broth, and water. Bring to a boil. Reduce heat; cover and simmer for 5 to 6 minutes or until rice is tender. Stir in water chestnuts, cranberries, onions, and soy sauce. Stuff into hens. Place on rack in shallow roasting pan. Bake at 375 degrees for 45 minutes. APRICOT GLAZE: In saucepan, combine butter, preserves, honey, onion, and nutmeg. Cook and stir until preserves are melted. Brush over hens; bake for 30 to 35 minutes longer or until juices run clear and meat thermometer inserted into stuffing reads 165 degrees. Let stand 5 minutes before serving.

Chicken Parmesan

MARINARA:
6 tablespoons olive oil
1/3 cup onion, finely diced
2 (14.5 ounce) cans crushed tomatoes
1 (6 ounce) can tomato paste
4 tablespoons fresh parsley, chopped
2 cloves garlic, minced
1 teaspoon dried oregano
1 teaspoon salt
1 tablespoon brown sugar
1/4 teaspoon ground black pepper
1/2 cup white wine

CHICKEN:
4 (4 ounce) boneless, skinless chicken
   breast halves
1/2 cup Italian-seasoned bread crumbs
1/4 cup parmesan cheese, grated
1/2 teaspoon dried basil
1 teaspoon garlic salt
1 egg
1 tablespoon butter
1 tablespoon olive oil
4 slices mozzarella cheese
Parsley (optional)

MARINARA: In large skillet, heat 6 tablespoons olive oil over medium heat; sauté onion for 2 minutes. Add rest of ingredients; simmer for 30 minutes, stirring occasionally. CHICKEN: Flatten chicken to ½-inch thickness. In shallow bowl, combine bread crumbs, parmesan cheese, basil, and garlic salt. In another bowl, beat egg. Dip chicken into egg, then coat with crumb mixture. In large skillet, brown chicken in butter and 1 tablespoon olive oil over medium heat. Place browned chicken in greased 13x9x2-inch baking dish. Top each chicken breast with slice of mozzarella cheese and spoon 2 tablespoons marinara over cheese slice. Bake at 350 degrees for 30 minutes or until juices run clear. Garnish with parsley, if desired.

Holiday Roast Turkey

1 (12 pound) whole turkey
6 tablespoons butter, divided
4 cups warm water
3 tablespoons chicken bouillon

2 tablespoons dried parsley
1 teaspoon garlic powder
2 tablespoons dried minced onion
2 tablespoons seasoning salt

Rinse and wash turkey. Discard giblets, or add to pan if they are anyone's favorites. Place turkey in dutch oven or roasting pan. Separate skin over breast to make little pockets. Put 3 tablespoons butter on both sides between skin and breast meat. This makes for very juicy breast meat. In medium bowl, combine water with bouillon. Stir in parsley, garlic powder, and minced onion. Pour over top of turkey. Sprinkle seasoning salt over turkey. Cover with foil; bake at 350 degrees for 3½ to 4 hours or until internal temperature of turkey reaches 180 degrees. Remove foil during last 45 minutes to brown turkey.

Notes

Brine for Turkey

Brining is an easy way to add flavor and moistness to a turkey.

½ gallon vegetable broth
½ gallon apple juice
¾ cup sea salt
1 tablespoon crushed dried rosemary

1 tablespoon dried sage
1 tablespoon dried thyme
1 tablespoon dried savory
1 gallon ice water

In large stockpot, combine vegetable broth, apple juice, sea salt, rosemary, sage, thyme, and savory. Bring to a boil, stirring frequently to be sure salt is dissolved. Remove from heat and let cool to room temperature. When broth mixture is cool, pour into clean, food-safe, 5-gallon bucket. Stir in ice water. Remove neck and giblets; wash and dry turkey. Place turkey, breast down, into brine, filling cavity. Place bucket in refrigerator overnight. Remove turkey carefully, draining off excess brine; rinse and pat dry. Discard excess brine. Cook turkey as desired, reserving the drippings for gravy. Keep in mind that brined turkeys cook 20 to 30 minutes faster, so watch the temperature gauge.

Notes

Chicken Cordon Bleu with Creamy Wine Sauce

The chicken is scrumptious and the sauce out of this world.
Serve this dish with garlic mashed potatoes and a salad or vegetable.

6 boneless, skinless chicken breast halves
2 tablespoons dijon mustard
½ pound swiss cheese, cut in logs
6 slices thin deli smoked ham
3 tablespoons flour
1 teaspoon paprika
2 eggs, beaten
½ cup panko bread crumbs

6 tablespoons butter
1 cup dry white wine
2 teaspoons chicken bouillon granules
2 tablespoons cornstarch
2 cups heavy whipping cream
Paprika (optional)
Parsley (optional)

Pound chicken breasts between sheets of waxed paper to ¼- to ½-inch thickness. Spread inside of chicken breast with thin layer of dijon mustard. Place cheese log in center of ham slice. Fold in edges and roll up. Place rolled-up ham in center of chicken breast. Fold edges of chicken over ham and roll up; secure with toothpicks. Mix flour and paprika in small bowl and coat chicken pieces. Dip in beaten eggs and roll in bread crumbs. Heat butter in large skillet over medium-high heat; cook chicken until browned on all sides. Remove toothpicks and place chicken in 9x13-inch greased baking dish and bake at 350 degrees for 35 minutes or until juices run clear. In same skillet over medium heat, mix wine and bouillon; deglaze pan. Blend cornstarch with cream in small bowl; whisk slowly into skillet. Cook sauce, stirring constantly until thickened. To serve, spoon sauce over chicken; sprinkle with paprika and parsley if desired.

Lasagna

1 pound sweet or mild Italian sausage
1 pound lean ground beef
½ cup onion, minced
2 cloves garlic, crushed
1 (28 ounce) can crushed tomatoes
2 (6 ounce) cans tomato paste
2 (6.5 ounce) cans tomato sauce
½ cup water
2 tablespoons sugar
1½ teaspoons dried basil leaves
½ teaspoon fennel seeds

1 teaspoon Italian seasoning
1½ teaspoons salt
¼ teaspoon ground black pepper
4 tablespoons fresh parsley, chopped, divided
12 lasagna noodles
16 ounces ricotta cheese
1 (8 ounce) package cream cheese, softened
2 eggs
1 pound mozzarella cheese, sliced
¾ cup grated parmesan cheese

Remove casing from sausage. In dutch oven, cook sausage, ground beef, onion, and garlic over medium heat until well browned. Stir in crushed tomatoes, tomato paste, tomato sauce, and water. Season with sugar, basil, fennel seeds, Italian seasoning, salt, pepper, and 2 tablespoons parsley. Simmer, covered, for about 1½ hours, stirring occasionally. Bring large pot of lightly salted water to a boil. Cook lasagna noodles in boiling water for 8 to 10 minutes. Drain noodles and rinse with cold water. In mixing bowl, combine ricotta cheese, cream cheese, eggs, and remaining parsley. To assemble, spread ¾ cup meat sauce in bottom of greased 9x13-inch baking dish. Arrange three noodles lengthwise over meat sauce. Spread with one-third of ricotta cheese mixture. Top with one-fourth of mozzarella cheese slices. Spoon ¾ cup meat sauce over mozzarella and sprinkle with ¼ cup parmesan cheese. Repeat layers and top with remaining mozzarella and parmesan cheese. Cover with foil. To prevent sticking, either spray foil with cooking spray or make sure foil does not touch cheese. Bake at 350 degrees for 30 minutes. Remove foil and bake an additional 25 minutes. Cool for 15 minutes before serving. *If you are short on time, brown meat and mix sauce ingredients but don't heat. While mixing sauce ingredients, soak lasagna noodles in very hot tap water for 20 minutes. Drain noodles and continue according to instructions. Refrigerate overnight. Bake covered 35 minutes and uncovered for 30 minutes.

Baked Tilapia

4 (6 ounce) tilapia fillets
3 tablespoons butter, melted
3 tablespoons lemon juice
1½ teaspoons garlic powder

⅛ teaspoon salt
2 tablespoons capers, drained
½ teaspoon dried dill
⅛ teaspoon paprika

Place tilapia in ungreased 9x13-inch baking dish. In small bowl, combine butter, lemon juice, garlic powder, and salt; pour over fillets. Sprinkle with capers, dill, and paprika. Bake uncovered at 425 degrees for 10 to 15 minutes or until fish flakes easily with a fork. Yield: 4 servings.

Tilapia with Dill Sauce

DILL SAUCE:
¼ cup mayonnaise
½ cup sour cream
⅛ teaspoon garlic powder
1 teaspoon fresh lemon juice
2 tablespoons fresh dill, chopped

TILAPIA:
1 tablespoon butter
1 tablespoon olive oil
4 (4 ounce) tilapia fillets
Salt and pepper to taste
1 tablespoon Old Bay seasoning
Fresh lemon wedge

DILL SAUCE: Mix mayonnaise, sour cream, garlic powder, lemon juice, and dill in small bowl. Refrigerate. TILAPIA: Heat butter and olive oil in skillet over medium heat. Sprinkle both sides of fillets with salt, pepper, and Old Bay seasoning; lay fillets in heated skillet. Sear fillets 2 to 4 minutes on each side, until the fish is golden brown on the outside and opaque and flaky inside. Serve with dill sauce and wedge of fresh lemon.

Chicken Potpie

2 deep-dish unbaked piecrusts
1 egg white, beaten, divided
1 pound boneless, skinless chicken breast
  halves, cubed
1 cup carrots, sliced
1 cup frozen green peas
½ cup celery, sliced
½ cup potato, peeled and diced
½ cup butter

⅓ cup onion, chopped
½ cup flour
½ teaspoon salt
¼ teaspoon black pepper
¼ teaspoon garlic powder
½ teaspoon poultry seasoning
¼ teaspoon celery seed
3 cups chicken broth
1⅓ cups milk

Place one unbaked crust in 9-inch deep-dish pie pan. Brush with egg white.

Set crust and remaining egg white aside. In saucepan, combine chicken,

carrots, peas, celery, and potato. Cover with water and boil for 15 minutes or until vegetables are tender. Remove from heat, drain, and set aside. In saucepan heat butter on medium; cook onion until soft and translucent. Stir in flour, salt, pepper, garlic powder, poultry seasoning, and celery seed. Slowly stir in chicken broth and milk. Simmer over medium-low heat until thick. Remove from heat. Combine chicken mixture with sauce mixture; spoon into prepared crust. Cover with top crust, seal edges, and cut away excess dough. Make several small slits in top to allow steam to escape. Brush with remaining egg white. Bake at 350 degrees for 45 minutes or until pastry is golden brown and filling is bubbly. Cool 10 minutes before serving.

Travison's Hearty Shepherd's Pie

1 pound ground beef
1 medium onion, chopped
2 cloves fresh garlic, minced
1 cup frozen baby beans
1 cup frozen baby carrots
1 cup frozen whole kernel corn
1 cup frozen peas
1 cup fresh mushrooms, sliced
1 (14.5 ounce) can diced tomatoes,
  undrained

1 (12 ounce) jar beef gravy
2 tablespoons chili sauce
½ teaspoon dried basil
⅛ teaspoon pepper
1 egg
3 cups leftover mashed potatoes
2 teaspoons parmesan cheese, shredded
Paprika

Cook ground beef and onion in 12-inch nonstick skillet over medium heat,

stirring occasionally, until beef is brown and onions are tender. Add garlic and brown another minute. Drain well. Stir in frozen vegetables, mushrooms, tomatoes, gravy, chili sauce, basil, and pepper. Heat to boiling; reduce heat. Cover and simmer about 10 minutes or until vegetables are tender. Spoon beef mixture into greased 8-inch baking dish or 2-quart casserole dish. In small bowl, whisk egg until well beaten. Mix mashed potatoes and beaten egg together; spoon over beef mixture. Sprinkle with cheese. Bake uncovered at 350 degrees for 25 to 30 minutes or until beef mixture is bubbly. Sprinkle with paprika if desired.

Notes

Pork Medallions

1 pork tenderloin
1 tablespoon olive or canola oil
1 tablespoon butter
1 small onion, thinly sliced
½ cup fresh mushrooms, sliced
2 garlic cloves, minced
1 tablespoon flour
½ cup chicken broth

½ cup dry white wine
1 teaspoon browning sauce
½ teaspoon dried rosemary, crushed
½ teaspoon dried savory
½ teaspoon salt
¼ teaspoon pepper
Minced fresh parsley

Slice tenderloin into ½-inch medallions. Add oil to skillet; brown pork for about 2 minutes on each side. Remove from skillet and set aside. In same skillet, melt butter. Add onion and mushrooms; sauté for 2 minutes. Add garlic and sauté 1 minute. Stir in flour until blended. Gradually stir in broth, wine, browning sauce, rosemary, savory, salt, and pepper. Bring to a boil; cook and stir for 1 minute or until thickened. Lay pork medallions over mixture. Reduce heat; cover and simmer for 10 to 15 minutes or until meat juices run clear. Garnish with parsley if desired.

Notes

Slow Cooker Pot Roast

While you're doing your Christmas shopping, supper can be cooking at home. It's perfect for a cold winter's night.

½ cup flour
½ teaspoon garlic salt
¼ teaspoon dried crushed rosemary
1 (5½ pound) pot roast
2 tablespoons butter

2 (10.75 ounce) cans condensed cream of mushroom soup
1 (1 ounce) package dry onion soup mix
1¼ cups water
½ cup barbecue sauce

In shallow bowl, mix flour, garlic salt, and rosemary. Dredge pot roast in flour mixture. Melt butter in skillet over medium heat. When butter is hot, sear top and bottom sides of pot roast in skillet until browned. Remove from skillet and place in slow cooker. In same skillet, mix cream of mushroom soup, dry onion soup mix, water, and barbecue sauce. Stir, deglazing bottom of skillet. Pour soup mixture over pot roast in slow cooker. Cook on high 3 to 4 hours or on low 8 to 9 hours. You can also add small red potatoes, carrots, sliced onion, or green beans if desired.

Notes

Sweet Treats: Cookies & Candy

Here's a fun idea for a holiday tradition: an old-fashioned Christmas tea. Send out invitations on cards with warm Christmas themes. Assign each guest a cookie or candy recipe found in this section (be sure to include the recipe in the invitation). Ask guests to bring the finished product on a pretty Christmas plate or glass pedestal cake holder for presentation.

Tea is usually held midafternoon with very light refreshments. Serve crustless finger sandwiches and a tray of fresh vegetables along with the candies and cookies. Place plates of food and treats all along the table and invite guests to serve themselves. Brew a few tea options and be sure to have a caffeine-free or herbal variety available. No tea bags allowed!

If you don't already own them, borrow a pretty selection of teapots, cream and sugar vessels, teaspoons, and small plates. An eclectic presentation of teacups and saucers is beautiful and fun, but few of us keep this kind of collection, so borrow pretty sets from friends.

If you wish, and if time allows, ask one of your guests who has agreed in advance to demonstrate a simple take on an intimidating candy recipe, such as fudge. This activity is a fun conclusion to tea and can be a big encouragement to candy-making novices. Keep the demonstration to twenty or thirty minutes at the most.

Other tips:

- Be sure to return all borrowed china, cleaned and well packed, within a day or two of your event.

- Serve real cream, sugar, and sliced lemons with tea. Old-fashioned sugar cubes are fun, too.

- Let each guest take home a selection of cookies and candy as a favor. Have Christmas storage bags available if needed.

Candy Bar Candy

This candy tastes like a candy bar you buy at the store, only with homemade flavor. Any batch you make sure won't last long.

CANDY:
2 tablespoons butter, softened
1 cup milk chocolate chips

¼ cup butterscotch chips
¼ cup creamy peanut butter

FILLING:
¼ cup butter
1 cup sugar
¼ cup evaporated milk
1½ cups marshmallow crème

¼ cup creamy peanut butter
1 teaspoon vanilla
1½ cups salted peanuts, chopped

CARAMEL LAYER:
1 (14 ounce) package caramels   ¼ cup whipping cream

ICING:
1 cup milk chocolate chips   ¼ cup creamy peanut butter
¼ cup butterscotch chips

. . . .

CANDY: Spread bottom and sides of 9x13-inch glass baking dish with butter. Combine chocolate chips, butterscotch chips, and peanut butter in small saucepan; stir over low heat until melted and smooth. Spread into prepared pan. Chill until set. FILLING: Melt butter in heavy saucepan over medium heat. Add sugar and milk; bring to a gentle boil. Reduce heat to medium-low; boil and stir for 5 minutes. Remove from heat; stir in marshmallow crème, peanut butter, and vanilla. Add peanuts. Spread over first layer. Chill until set. CARAMEL LAYER: Combine caramels and cream in saucepan; stir over low heat until melted and smooth. Cook and stir 4 minutes longer. Spread over filling. Chill until set. ICING: In another saucepan, combine chips and peanut butter; stir over low heat until melted and smooth. Pour over caramel layer. Chill for at least 4 hours. Remove from refrigerator 20 minutes before cutting. Cut into 1-inch squares.

Caramel-Filled Chocolate Cookies

2½ cups flour
¾ cup cocoa
1 teaspoon baking soda
1 cup sugar
1 cup brown sugar
1 cup butter

2 teaspoons vanilla
2 eggs
1 cup pecans, chopped, divided
48 caramel-filled chocolate candies
1 tablespoon sugar
4 ounces white chocolate

In small bowl, combine flour, cocoa, and baking soda; blend well. In large bowl, beat 1 cup sugar, brown sugar, and butter until light and fluffy. Add vanilla and eggs; beat well. Add flour mixture; blend well. Stir in ½ cup pecans. With floured hands, shape about 1 tablespoon dough around 1 caramel candy, covering completely. In small bowl, combine remaining ½ cup pecans and 1 tablespoon sugar. Press one side of each ball into pecan mixture. Place, nut side up, 2 inches apart on ungreased cookie sheets. Bake at 375 degrees for 7 to 10 minutes or until set and slightly cracked. Cool 2 minutes, then remove from cookie sheets. Cool completely. Melt white chocolate in microwave. Drizzle over cookies.

Notes

Cranberry Chip Cookies

The combination of the tart cranberries, sweet white chocolate, and crunchy walnuts is a delightful mixture of flavors and textures.

½ cup butter, softened
½ cup shortening
¾ cup sugar
¾ cup brown sugar
2 eggs
1 teaspoon vanilla
2¼ cups flour

1 teaspoon baking soda
½ teaspoon salt
1 cup white chocolate chips
1 cup dried cranberries
1 cup walnuts, chopped
Additional white chocolate chips
    for drizzling, if desired

In mixing bowl, cream butter, shortening, and sugars. Add eggs, one at a time, beating well after each addition. Beat in vanilla. Combine flour, baking soda, and salt; gradually add to creamed mixture. Stir in white chocolate chips, cranberries, and walnuts. Drop by tablespoonfuls 2 inches apart onto ungreased baking sheets. Bake at 375 degrees for 9 to 11 minutes or until golden brown. Cool for 2 minutes before removing to wire racks. Drizzle with melted white chocolate, if desired.

Notes

Frosted Cashew Cookies

*When you top these cookies with a salted pecan half,
they have the perfect blend of sweet and salty.*

COOKIES:
½ cup butter, softened
1 cup brown sugar
1 egg
⅓ cup sour cream
½ teaspoon vanilla

2 cups flour
¾ teaspoon baking powder
¾ teaspoon baking soda
¾ teaspoon salt
1¾ cups salted cashew halves

BROWNED BUTTER FROSTING:
½ cup butter
3 tablespoons half-and-half
¼ teaspoon vanilla

2 cups powdered sugar
Cashew halves (optional)

COOKIES: In mixing bowl, cream butter and brown sugar. Beat in egg, sour cream, and vanilla; mix well. Combine dry ingredients except cashews; add to creamed mixture and mix well. Fold in cashews. Drop by teaspoonfuls 2 inches apart onto greased baking sheets. Bake at 375 degrees for 8 to 10 minutes or until lightly browned. Remove to wire racks to cool. BROWNED BUTTER FROSTING: Lightly brown butter in small saucepan. Remove from heat; add half-and-half and vanilla. Beat in powdered sugar until smooth and thick. Frost cookies. Top each with a salted cashew half, if desired.

Notes

....

....

Monster Cookies

Who doesn't love these chewy, peanut buttery, candy-filled cookies?
Because they make such a large batch, consider freezing some to use
on unexpected cookie trays. When making these for the holidays,
use red and green candy-coated chocolates to make them look more festive.

½ pound butter, softened
6 eggs
1½ cups brown sugar
1¼ cups white sugar
4 teaspoons soda
1 teaspoon corn syrup

1 teaspoon vanilla
1½ pounds peanut butter
9 cups quick oats
½ pound candy-coated milk chocolate
pieces
½ pound semisweet chocolate chips

In large mixing bowl, cream together butter and eggs. Add sugars, soda, corn syrup, vanilla, and peanut butter; mix well. Stir in oats, candy-coated milk chocolate pieces, and chocolate chips. Use an ice cream scoop to drop onto baking sheets. Bake at 350 degrees for 12 to 15 minutes or until lightly browned. Do not overbake.

Notes

White Chocolate Raspberry Cookies

8 ounces white chocolate baking bars, divided
½ cup butter, softened
1 cup sugar
1 teaspoon baking soda
¼ teaspoon salt

2 large eggs
2¾ cups flour
½ cup seedless raspberry jam
3 ounces white chocolate baking bars
½ teaspoon vegetable shortening

Chop 4 ounces white chocolate. Set aside. In heavy small saucepan, heat another 4 ounces white chocolate over low heat until melted, stirring constantly; cool. In large mixing bowl, beat butter with electric mixer on medium to high speed for 30 seconds. Add sugar, baking soda, and salt; beat until combined. Beat in eggs and melted white baking bars until combined.

Stir in flour until just combined. Fold in 4 ounces chopped white chocolate. Drop dough by rounded teaspoonfuls about 2 inches apart onto greased cookie sheet. Press thumb in top of ball slightly to make indentation for jam. Bake at 375 degrees for 7 to 9 minutes or until edges are lightly browned. Cool on cookie sheet 1 minute. Transfer to wire rack to cool completely. In small saucepan, heat raspberry jam over low heat until melted. Spoon about ½ teaspoon jam onto top of each cookie. In heavy small saucepan, combine 3 ounces white chocolate and shortening. Heat over low heat until melted, stirring constantly. Drizzle over cookies in a decorative manner. Allow chocolate to set before serving or storing.

Tasha's Snickerdoodles

Try a festive variation by dividing the dough in three equal parts. Add green food coloring to one part, red to another, and leave the third one plain. Then roll each part in a rope and braid the three together. Pinch off enough of the braid to form a 1-inch ball and then roll it in the cinnamon sugar. The end result is red, green, and cream-colored cookies.

½ cup butter, softened
1½ cups sugar
2 eggs
1 teaspoon vanilla
2¾ cups flour

1 teaspoon cream of tartar
½ teaspoon baking soda
¼ teaspoon salt
2 tablespoons sugar
2 teaspoons cinnamon

Cream together butter and sugar until light and fluffy. Add eggs and vanilla;

beat well. Combine flour, cream of tartar, baking soda, and salt. Stir into butter mixture until well blended and smooth. Mix additional sugar and cinnamon. Pull off pieces of dough and roll into 1-inch balls. Roll balls in cinnamon sugar and place on baking sheet about 2½ inches apart. Bake at 400 degrees for 8 to 10 minutes or until cookies are light golden brown. Let cookies cool slightly on baking sheet. Remove and let cool completely.

Notes

Chocolate-Covered Cherry Cookies

½ cup butter
1 cup sugar
1 egg
1½ teaspoons vanilla extract
1½ cups flour
½ cup unsweetened cocoa powder

¼ teaspoon salt
¼ teaspoon baking soda
¼ teaspoon baking powder
1 (10 ounce) jar maraschino cherries
¼ cup sweetened condensed milk
½ cup semisweet chocolate chips

Beat butter and sugar together in bowl. Add egg and vanilla and beat well. Add flour, cocoa powder, salt, baking soda, and baking powder and stir until smooth. Roll mixture into 1-inch balls about the size of a walnut (larger if desired). Place on ungreased cookie sheets. Press center of each ball with thumb. Drain cherries and reserve juice. Place cherry in indentation of each cookie ball. Bake at 350 degrees for 8 to 10 minutes or until set. In saucepan, heat condensed milk and chocolate chips until chips are melted. Stir in 2 tablespoons cherry juice. Spoon about 1 teaspoon of mixture over each cherry and spread to cover cherry. Cool completely.

Notes

Chocolate Malt Cookies

1 cup butter-flavored shortening
1¼ cups brown sugar
½ cup malted milk powder
2 tablespoons chocolate syrup
1 tablespoon vanilla
1 egg

2 cups flour
1 teaspoon baking soda
½ teaspoon salt
1½ cups semisweet chocolate chunks
1 cup milk chocolate chips

In mixing bowl, combine shortening, brown sugar, malted milk powder, chocolate syrup, and vanilla. Beat 2 minutes, scraping sides of bowl periodically. Add egg; beat well. In separate bowl, combine flour, baking soda, and salt; gradually add to creamed mixture. Mix well. Stir in chocolate chunks and chips. Shape into 2-inch balls and place 3 inches apart on ungreased cookie sheets. Bake at 375 degrees for 12 to 15 minutes or until golden brown. Cool for 2 minutes before removing to wire rack.

Notes

....

....

....

....

....

Banana Oatmeal Cookies

*These melt-in-your-mouth banana cookies are a great solution
for overripe bananas. They are delightful after they have
been rolled in the powdered sugar and are still warm.*

¾ cup butter, softened
1 cup sugar
1 egg
1 teaspoon vanilla
1 cup ripe banana, mashed
1½ cups flour
1 teaspoon salt

½ teaspoon baking soda
¼ teaspoon nutmeg
¼ teaspoon cinnamon
1¾ cups quick oatmeal
½ cup walnuts or pecans, chopped
Powdered sugar

In large mixing bowl, cream together butter and sugar until light and fluffy. Add egg, vanilla, and mashed banana; beat well. Combine flour, salt, baking soda, nutmeg, and cinnamon; add to creamed mixture and mix. Stir in oatmeal and nuts. Drop dough by teaspoonfuls onto greased cookie sheet about 2 inches apart. Bake at 350 degrees for 10 to 12 minutes. Do not overbake. Remove from baking sheet and roll in powdered sugar while still hot. Let them cool slightly and roll in powdered sugar a second time.

Notes

Mom's Old-Fashioned Peanut Brittle

1½ cups sugar
⅔ cup water
⅔ cup light corn syrup
2 tablespoons butter
1 cup raw Spanish peanuts

½ teaspoon salt
½ teaspoon vanilla extract
½ teaspoon baking soda
1½ teaspoons water

Grease large cookie sheet. Set aside. In heavy 2-quart saucepan, over medium heat, bring to a boil sugar, ⅔ cup water, and corn syrup. Stir until sugar is dissolved. Set candy thermometer in place and continue cooking. Stir frequently until temperature reaches 250 degrees. Stir in butter and peanuts and continue to boil to 300 degrees or until small amount of mixture dropped into very cold water separates into hard and brittle threads. Remove from heat. Mix together with two forks; lift and pull peanut mixture into rectangle about 14x12 inches; cool. Snap candy into salt, vanilla, baking soda, and 1½ teaspoons water. Mix well and fast. Pour at once onto large greased cookie sheet.

Notes

Coconut Cashew Brittle

2 tablespoons plus 1 cup butter, divided
2 cups cashew halves
2 cups flaked coconut
2 cups sugar

1 cup light corn syrup
½ cup plus 1 teaspoon water, divided
2 teaspoons vanilla
1½ teaspoons baking soda

Butter two 15x10x1-inch pans each with 1 tablespoon butter; set aside.
Combine cashews and coconut on 15x10x1-inch baking pan. Bake at 350
degrees for 8 to 10 minutes or until golden brown, stirring occasionally. In
large heavy saucepan, combine sugar, corn syrup, and ½ cup water. Cook and
stir over medium heat until mixture comes to a boil. Add remaining butter;
cook and stir until butter is melted. Continue cooking, without stirring,
until candy thermometer reads 300 degrees (hard-crack stage). Meanwhile,

combine vanilla, baking soda, and remaining water. Remove saucepan from heat; add cashews and coconut. Stir in baking soda mixture. Quickly pour onto prepared baking sheets. Spread with buttered metal spatula to ¼-inch thickness. Cool before breaking into pieces. Store in airtight container.

Notes

English Toffee

These make a pretty addition to a holiday tray.
The crunchy butter treat is also wonderful given as a gift.

2 cups butter
2 cups sugar
⅓ cup water
2 tablespoons light-colored corn syrup

1¾ cups milk chocolate pieces
1 cup toasted nuts (almonds, pecans, walnuts, and/or cashews), finely chopped

Line 15x10x1-inch baking pan with foil, extending the foil over edges of pan. Set baking pan aside. In 3-quart saucepan, melt butter. Stir in sugar, water, and corn syrup. Cook over medium-high heat to boiling, stirring until sugar is dissolved. Avoid splashing side of saucepan. Carefully clip candy thermometer to pan. Cook over medium heat, stirring frequently, until thermometer registers 290 degrees, soft-crack stage (about 15 minutes). Mixture should boil at a moderate, steady rate with bubbles over entire surface. Remove from heat; remove thermometer. Carefully pour mixture into prepared pan; spread evenly. Cool about 5 minutes or until top is set. Sprinkle with chocolate pieces; let stand 2 minutes. Spread softened chocolate over candy. Sprinkle with nuts; press into chocolate. Let stand at room temperature several hours or until set. Use foil to lift candy out of pan; break into pieces.

Notes

....

....

Peanut Butter Fudge

4 cups white sugar
1 cup light brown sugar
½ cup butter
1 (12 ounce) can evaporated milk

1 (7 ounce) jar marshmallow crème
1 (16 ounce) jar peanut butter
1 teaspoon vanilla

In medium saucepan over medium heat, combine sugar, brown sugar, butter, and evaporated milk. Bring to a boil, stirring constantly. When it begins to boil, stop stirring and let it continue to boil until temperature reaches soft ball stage (235 to 240 degrees). Remove from heat; stir in marshmallow crème until well incorporated and melted. Let cool slightly. Stir in peanut butter and vanilla until smooth; spread in greased 9x13-inch pan. Let cool before cutting into squares.

Notes

....

....

....

....

....

....

....

Soft Cutout Cookies

COOKIES:
1 cup butter, softened
1 cup sugar
1 cup brown sugar
3 eggs
1 cup heavy cream

1 teaspoon salt
1 teaspoon baking soda
5 teaspoons baking powder
1 teaspoon vanilla
5 cups flour

FROSTING:
3 cups powdered sugar
½ cup butter, softened

1 teaspoon vanilla
¼ cup milk

COOKIES: In large mixing bowl, cream butter and sugars until light and fluffy.
Beat in eggs and heavy cream. Add salt, baking soda, baking powder, vanilla,

and flour; mix well. Chill dough for several hours. Roll out dough on lightly floured surface with rolling pin. Roll to ½-inch thickness. Dip cookie cutters in flour prior to cutting dough. Bake at 350 degrees for approximately 10 to 12 minutes or until lightly colored. Do not overbake. FROSTING: Mix frosting ingredients together until creamy. Frost cooled cookies.

Notes

Creative Traditions for All Ages

Christmas is a time for merriment and cheer, but that doesn't mean that you have to celebrate the same way year after year! Here are some creative and fun ideas to incorporate into the holiday season. Remember that these are just starting points. Feel free to take these ideas and make them your own!

At Christmas, play and make good cheer,
For Christmas comes but once a year.

THOMAS TUSSER, 16TH CENTURY

Notes

....

....

....

....

....

....

....

Cookie Share

ITEMS NEEDED:
Cookie recipes
Ingredients
Icing and other decorations

Festive disposable plates
Holiday plastic wrap

Cookie baking is one of those yearly events that's a great way to get the whole family busy in the kitchen. Maybe it's a special time for multiple generations, the extended family, or a small affair with just members of your household. The mixing, preparing, baking, and decorating is not only fun—it's tasty, too!

In addition to the cookie plates you may be making for friends, neighbors, and family, consider baking some extra cookies to share with local ministries that could use some Christmas cheer. Consider women's or homeless shelters, nursing homes, or other local charities that help individuals. You could also share a plate of cookies with the local firehouse or police department or other public servants.

If your baking festivities include children, take them along to deliver the treats. It's a great way to teach love in action to the next generation.

And the angel said unto them, Fear not: for, behold,
I bring you good tidings of great joy,
which shall be to all people.
LUKE 2:10

Gingerbread House Contest

ITEMS NEEDED:
Aluminum Foil
1 (8x8 inch) piece of cardboard per house
Scotch tape
1 sleeve graham crackers per house

1 gallon-size resealable bag of icing
  per house
Multicolored candy of all sorts
Kitchen timer

Even people who don't bake or craft the rest of the year seem to enjoy getting creative during the Christmas season. Here's a fun and festive way to introduce a little spirited competition in your celebrations.

Divide into teams. Usually teams of two or three work best. Provide each team with a cardboard square to cover with foil and secure with scotch tape. Give each team 1 sleeve of graham crackers and a gallon resealable bag with Gingerbread House Icing* in it (instruct them to cut a small hole in the corner of the bag and use it like a piping bag to put the house together and decorate it). The icing will set and harden, acting as a glue to hold the house together and hold decorative candy in place.

Set a kitchen timer for a predetermined amount of time and watch the creative juices flow. After the completion of the construction and decoration, have an impartial judge determine the winner. Or, instead of awarding places, have the judge make up categories so that every house can be recognized ("Most Creative Use of Candy Canes," "Best Architectural Features," "Hansel and Gretel Look-Alike").

*Gingerbread House Icing

1 pound powdered sugar
1 teaspoon cream of tartar

3 egg whites

Beat all ingredients until very stiff. Use as glue for assembling house. Icing will harden as it sits, so add a few drops of water as needed.

Kids' Holiday Games

Christmas Musical Chairs: Use a CD of kids' Christmas music and play traditional Musical Chairs.

Fill the Stocking: Divide into two teams lined up across the room from two hung Christmas stockings. A bowl of wrapped candy and a spoon are placed at the head of each line. In relay fashion, the children take turns carrying a candy on the spoon, depositing it in the stocking and running back to hand the spoon off to the next person in line. The first team to deposit a predetermined number of candies in the stocking wins!

Christmas Twenty Questions: Have everyone sit in a circle with a bowl of candy in the middle. Going around the circle, kids take turns asking the hostess two or three questions and then taking a guess about what the answer is from a simple list of things or people pertaining to the Christmas season. When anyone guesses correctly, he gets to choose a piece of candy from the bowl. Let every child choose a piece of candy when the game is over.

Notes

Christmas Greetings

Christmas Prayers: Create an area in your kitchen or dining area where you can display the Christmas cards that you receive during the holiday season. Every time you eat together as a family, choose a card and pray a special Christmas blessing for the senders of the card.

Card Day: Instead of buying premade Christmas cards, consider making them yourself out of decorative scrapbook paper, stickers, multicolored pens, glitter, and old holiday cards. Spend the whole day as a family designing and creating unique cards for friends, neighbors, family, teachers, and other special people in your life. This is especially fun for kids to get involved in, and it's something they will remember for years to come.

Christmas News: Holiday greetings are a great opportunity to share the latest news and updates about your family, but instead of typing out a wordy newsletter about the who, what, when, where, and why of each member of your family, give them each the opportunity to write down one thing they would like to share with the recipients of this year's cards. Let everyone use their creativity—maybe it will be a simple greeting or some bit of news or accomplishment or an original poem or joke about the season. Let the individuality of your family members shine through.

Notes

....

....

....

The Twelve Days of Christmas

Keep the joy of Christmas going in your house for nearly two weeks after Christmas by following this guide:

December 26: Family game night

December 27: Do something nice for someone else

December 28: Dinner out at a restaurant

December 29: After-Christmas sales shopping

December 30: Write and send thank-you notes

December 31: New Year's Eve celebrations

January 1: Pizza dinner while taking down the Christmas tree

January 2: Family game night

January 3: Movie night, watching a favorite Christmas movie and eating popcorn

January 4: Bake cookies and enjoy hot chocolate
January 5: Kids choose the menu tonight
January 6: Celebrate Epiphany by taking dinner to a shut-in from church

The time of year when all things seem to don a friendly glow,
When children's eyes are filled with dreams of stockings in a row.

A time of year for strings of lights and manger scenes nearby,
For candlelight and Christmas trees and songs in rich supply.

COLEEN L. REECE & JULIE REECE-DEMARCO

Caroling, Caroling

Here's a simple tradition that spans centuries and unites cultures from all over the globe. Choose an evening to spread joy through song. Caroling can be done as a family or as a large group that includes family, friends, neighbors, church choir members—everyone can make a joyful Christmas noise!

Prepare a song list in advance and create a lyrics sheet for carolers to carry with them as they sing. It's important to choose familiar songs and sing only the most well-known verses of the songs so that anyone feels free to join in.

In addition to shut-ins or elderly people still living at home, consider caroling at retirement homes or rehabilitation facilities as well as hospitals or a children's hospital (make sure to check in advance with these places so that you can follow their protocol concerning visitors and get special permission if necessary).

After an evening of caroling, enjoy a potluck dinner as a group or enjoy cookies and hot chocolate and celebrate the season.

Song list:
We Wish You a Merry Christmas
Away in a Manger
Jingle Bells
Joy to the World
Hark the Herald Angels Sing
Deck the Halls

Name That Tune

ITEMS NEEDED:
Christmas music   Pencil
CD player   Scorekeeper
Notepad

Select ten popular Christmas songs and play just a small portion of the song or edit snippets of the songs in various places. The first person to call out the right answer gets a point. Whoever gets the most songs right wins. Play just for fun or play for a prize.

Select a mix of traditional Christmas carols and popular Christmas songs ranging from easy to more difficult. Here are some ideas to keep everyone guessing:

- Ding Dong Merrily on High
- Let It Snow
- The Twelve Days of Christmas
- Angels We Have Heard on High
- Joy to the World
- Sleigh Ride
- I'll Be Home for Christmas
- Winter Wonderland
- Little Drummer Boy

A "Scrambled" Dinner Party

Invite about eight friends over for a casual dinner. Assign each couple one side dish recipe you plan to serve (enough for each guest to have a small serving). That's all they need to know. The host provides an entrée and dessert, but your guests won't have any idea what you're serving or what anyone else is bringing.

The night of the party, there are no place settings; the only items for each guest are a menu and a pen. Create the menus by folding paper in half like a greeting card. When opened, the left side of the menu will be a list of every item on the menu (including eating utensils, each individual dish, and beverage), but each will be cleverly disguised under a new name. Mashed potatoes become "Clouds over Bethlehem," and a butter knife is "Herod's Scepter." If your main dish is beef, you might call it "Cattle Are Lowing," a napkin is "Swaddling Clothes," and so on—pull out all your creative genius for this! The right side of the menu contains blank lines under the headings of Course I, Course II, Course III, one line for each item they'll be served from the left side of the menu. Have guests fill out all three courses at once then write their names at the top and turn them in to servers.

You will need help in the kitchen for this event, so ask a few of the members of the church youth group to come help out for this fun evening. They will be filling orders, serving, and clearing after each course. (Forget the good china and use fun holiday paper products and plastic utensils for quick cleanup.)

The fun really starts when Course I appears. Someone gets a vegetable, dessert, and meat but didn't order a fork, so she only has a toothpick to eat it with! Someone else has unwittingly ordered a napkin, a glass of water, and all his silverware for Course I and has to eat his next two courses with his fingers!

When the meal is over, invite guests to finish off any of the food, drink, and dessert left in the kitchen, this time filling their own plates.

Happy Birthday, Jesus!

Hold a kids-only birthday party for Jesus. Invite as many as you can handle, and make sure you have enough adult help. Ask each child to bring along a baked Christmas dessert in a disposable container that will be taken to a local retirement center. Make or buy a large Christmas greeting card on which every child can sign, draw a picture, or write a message to the folks at the retirement center.

Decorate for Jesus' birthday with balloons, streamers, party hats, noisemakers, and party plates and napkins. Bake a cake and add as many candles as there are kids at the party. Remind children that Jesus' birth made it possible for us to be reborn! Then gather the kids around to sing "Happy Birthday" to Jesus and blow out the candles together and enjoy cake and ice cream.

A nativity scene makes an excellent centerpiece for this party. Read a short, modern version of the Christmas story while the kids are seated.

Play Christmas-themed games (see examples in this book).

As the party comes to a close, join hands in a circle and sing a Christmas carol or other seasonal song together. Children love to sing!

The merry family gatherings—
the old, the very young;
the strangely lovely way they
harmonize in carols sung.
For Christmas is tradition time—
traditions that recall
the precious memories down the
years, the sameness of them all.

HELEN LOWRIE MARSHALL

Hide the Ornament

ITEM NEEDED:
1 unique ornament

Several cultures have the tradition of hiding an ornament (like a pickle) on the Christmas tree, and the first person to find it receives a special present. For your party, consider hiding a unique (or silly) ornament somewhere in your house that guests will have access to. As people arrive, explain the game to them and describe the ornament that they will be looking for. As the evening progresses, if no one finds the ornament, you can start dropping subtle hints about where it might be. When someone finds the ornament, they should be declared the winner and given a prize. If the ornament itself is especially strange (and doesn't hold sentimental value to you or your family) you may consider giving the ornament to the winner as it would make for a fun memory on their Christmas tree for years to come.

The pickle ornament is a very old German Christmas tradition. The parents hung the pickle last after all the other ornaments were in place and would give an extra present to the most observant child who found the pickle first. Why a pickle? Nobody knows exactly, but a dark green vegetable hidden deep inside a dark green tree makes for a challenging game!

Christmas Carol Pictionary

ITEMS NEEDED:

Paper
Pencil or pen
Hat or bowl

Whiteboard
Dry-erase markers

Have each player write the name of a Christmas carol on a small piece of paper. Fold each piece and place them in the hat or bowl. Teams must select an artist and draw clues to get the team to figure out the answer. If the team guesses the correct answer, they get a point. If that team doesn't guess, the opposing team gets one guess. Bonus points for the team that sings the entire song together!

Did You Know?

One of our most cherished Christmas carols is "Joy to the World." The lyrics were written by Sir Isaac Watts in the early 1700s, and the melody was composed by Lowell Mason. It is said that Watts never intended this to be a "Christmas" song, but a paraphrase of Psalm 98: "Make a joyful noise unto the LORD, all the earth. . . . For he cometh. . . ." (verses 4, 9).

White Chocolate Holiday Fruitcake Mix

Jar mixes are a fun, useful, and delicious favor to give to friends and neighbors as a special holiday treat. Here's a traditional Christmas dessert with a twist.

JAR PREPARATION:
- ½ cup brown sugar, packed
- 1⅓ cups flour
- 2 teaspoons baking powder
- ¼ teaspoon salt
- 6 ounces white chocolate baking bar, chopped
- ½ cup cashews, chopped
- ⅔ cup coconut, shredded
- ⅓ cup candied orange peel, diced
- ½ cup macadamia nuts, chopped
- ¼ cup dried cranberries

In a 1-quart widemouthed jar, layer ingredients in order given, combining flour, baking powder, and salt. Attach a recipe card with the following instructions (see next page).

Notes

....

....

....

....

....

White Chocolate Holiday Fruitcake

¼ cup butter, softened   3 large eggs

Preheat oven to 300 degrees. Grease a 9x5x3-inch loaf pan; line with waxed paper. Grease and flour waxed paper. Carefully remove white chocolate, nuts, coconut, orange peel, cranberries, and from White Chocolate Holiday Fruitcake Mix. In large mixing bowl, beat butter until fluffy. Add eggs and beat well. Add remaining contents of fruitcake mix in jar, beating on low speed until well blended. Fold in white chocolate, nuts, and fruit. Batter will be very thick and chunky. Spoon batter into prepared pan. Bake 1 hour and 15 minutes. Run sharp knife around edge of pan to loosen fruitcake; cool in pan on wire rack for 30 minutes. Invert to wire rack and cool completely.